footnote to *silence*

FOOTNOTE TO *SILENCE*

Ars Cogitanda

gnOme

gnOme books
gnomebooks.wordpress.com

Please address inquiries to:
gnomebooks@gmail.com

Cover image source: http://en.wikipedia.org/wiki/Lucy (Australopithecus)#mediaviewer/File:Lucy_blackbg.jpg [CC BY 2.5]

ISBN-13: 978-0692352311
ISBN-10: 0692352317

A portion of this work was previously published in *filling Station*, Issue 59 (http://www.fillingstation.ca/)

With respect to Isabel, Alexandria, the Newton Advisory
and the rest of the body politic

.

FOOTNOTE TO *SILENCE*

The assembled footnoters wish to acknowledge their partial understanding: imperceptibility will be modified; silence spatially articulated. Other than that no claim can be made beyond contextual enactments.

<u>material evaluation</u> | <u>"**thing**ness"</u>

Notation || regarding the section
Identity position coalesces under nomina **thing** |
identifiers include |

___evidence of temporal lobe epilepsy
   time distortions present spatially
   , often in colour
   , sometimes as parallel streams of no**thing**
___recurrent rem sleep images, for example, black rabbit
   | hunts words with a broccoli spear
   , for example, red/white caves
   , CaCo$_3$ bones, trilobite fossils breaking stone
   , water running white
___perceptual anomalies, as in, time | smells
   of moonstone, night, intensity
   , as in
   limbic floods in the range [emr frequencies
   ~ 390nm to 700nm]

[1] In this part of THE TEXT, the simple story of a primate requiring imprinting by its environment in order to develop language, and selfhood enacts. The specifics acquired by the flow of events that trigger relevant (predisposed) neuronal pathways result in the development (inscription) of complexes of related pathways. The primate experiences (enacts) (edits inscription) variously and simultaneously as "language" and as one or more "self".

[2] Defining "a **thing**" is contentious. The article "a", implies non-specific singularity. As THE TEXT makes clear, this is an inaccurate representation. Further, since there is no foundational reference to which a fact may refer, "a **thing**" cannot appeal to singularity. In this way, identity partakes in the contextualization of **thing**-relations (enacts &/or edits inscription).

3 **Thing**: [here defined] a rush of colour between two steep banks of no**thing**.

4 For specificities sake, Sinoburius lunaris is the fossil form most common in the the (cognitive) environs of THE TEXT. The kinship relationship ascribed has as much elasticity as does the definition of the term **thing**.

5 Primate evolutionary history requires environmental triggers in order to enable post-partum development (including the development of the here-gathered footnoters). Specifically, the dependence upon social structures to foster genetic survival of individual lineages sets up consequences. One of those results in a sequence of imprinting events in which the infant gains the necessary sequence of learned responses that will enable social, lingustic, psychological competence. The developing complex of these various neurological-behavioural networks encapsulates imagistically under the nomina "self".

6 **Thing**: [here defined] as sensory image enacted through contextual reference on the world (through its moments of instantiation) rather than on human or other animal beings.

7 While the literature has been slow to accept that human-instantiated forms are nevertheless animal instantiated forms, some acceptance, of late, has been noticed with respect to the use of the terms "instinct" and "imprint" as applied to the formation of neurological correlates of social learning complexes. An instance not mentioned by THE TEXT, but written about elsewhere by the authorial construct (A-C), are the neurological "mutations" made possible by human imprinting on non-human or non-living instantiations in the biosocial world of infants and young children. THE TEXT, on this subject, in this footnoter's opinion, has yet to develop a comfortable

clarity. Partly, of course, this may be because THE TEXT is also undergoing mutation. This subject will be discussed further in section III and IV.

[8] The terminology and distinction between "**thing**" and "object" references Brown, Bill (2001). "**Thing** Theory". Critical Inquiry. v.28 n.1: pp.1-22. Having said that, this footnoter would suggest that an interested reader also reference *Zuhandenheit* and *Vorhandenheit* (Heidegegger's "present-at-hand" and "readiness-to-hand".) It is felt that all these categories reflect affordances (see later sections of this text) specific to human enactments of awareness as an emergent property of encephalization.

[9] Image: [here defined] sensory enactment of contextual attention of the cellular (in animals, including the neurological), and the framing of positionally acquired information.

[10] The appropriate question would be: Is silence a **thing** or a **thing**-in-relation?

[11] As examplars of other poetry fragments to be found in this text: **thing**ness: nose and other lives wriggle; earthworms mouth earth; fingers uncurl to palm air. It is not known if the authorial context exemplified irony; or a more simple acknowledgment of interacting forms of the "i".

[12] In other words, chemical constructs are simultaneously **thing**s and objects – objecthood is a reference to the construct from within its set of affordances – **thing**hood is a reference to the construct from the point of view of its place in the system which sustains the construct's ability to continue with its relative stability. It is likely that all constructs maintain the ability to shift between these referential states, in much the same way as a geographer

can switch between Euclidean and Geodesic references. Otherwise a construct that earns its living mapping the world couldn't walk the flat plain whilst creating a map of a that same plain in the context of a curved earth. In the case of a bird, there might not be the level of consciousness [here defined] as aware-self-referentiality and mutability-of-decision-making with reference to planning behavioural sets] but the bird must be able to both fly long distances (and thereby reference a geodesic model) and walk across the road to get to the other side (and thereby behaviourally referencing standard Euclidean concepts such as angles and lengths of line segments).

13 We refer readers to the seminal study "K is mentally ill: An anatomy of a factual account" by Dorothy E Smith.

14 The story presented in this paragraph resulted in a poem published as "intermittent".

15 Gravity and the occult! [at least 3 dashes of snigger, and boil with the wings of a guffaw {and yes, this footnoter admits the unfairness of such a response but really! (renewed sniggering)}]. [This accusation was leveled against Newton's notion of gravity by Leibniz because of the quote "gravity works on all bodies universally and is proportional to the quantity of matter in each" | note from another, more level-headed footnoter.]

16 We are all in agreement that the use of Tarot cards to speak to positional information was an unfortunate choice. It unnecessarily undermines critical discourse on the importance of positionally acquired information with respect to meaning construction, inscription and the process of spatial articulation of conceptual material. Accusations of "magic" are, while impertinent, and eventually just silly, nevertheless presently harmful due

largely to obfuscation of barely understood material process.

[17] Naming is otherwise the practice of transforming a **thing** into an object.

[18] "Gertrude during her living scuttled around on the floor of a shallow sea, probably a non-dominant member of a dominant species. Of course she didn't have the recurring promise of homelessness, but still, there is some**thing** about her mildly cockroach/human-like ubiquity that apparently stirs us (A-C to you) into empathy. As a matter of interest Gertrude, at the moment of initial taphonic conversion from living chemical construct (aka trilobite) to a what would become a pendant some 260 million years later, happend to be in exactly the right place – at the wrong time – so that a form of her survived the geologic processes of burial that both killed her and kept her body intact enough to fossilize. The billions of her kin over the many years before and after had different fortunes. They got blown apart, legs everywhich way. Their chemical consitutents are just the molecules in your morning tea." (personal communication)

[19] While it is possible that "red & white" reference alchemical geometrical constructs, the footnoters are more inclined to posit an affinity to certain mineral inclusions in material expressions of geologic processes. [We would like it to be known that we are not impressed with the A-C's tendency to cite arcane magical thought systems.]

[20] Silence [here defined]: the ephemeral text as an object, or ready-to-hand.

[21] We do not concur. However, we will agree that sensory overload represents a childhood haunt in both the spatial and temporal sense. We would prefer the referent of "i" to

be the factual account of existence. Since THE TEXT does not allow for a meaningful foundation for facts, and yet remains fiercely material, we are left with not only inexact limits, but mobile limits that precede to infinity.

22 Time | geologic & deep | moonstone and jet are also exemplars of silence.

23 Limbic floods: the authorial construct really means "feelings" and is referencing the eTEXT, in this context, known as, somatic signaling.

24 The full quote (Brown, 2001): "Temporalized as the before and after of the object, **thing**ness amounts to a latency (the not yet formed or the not yet formable) and to an excess (what remains physically or metaphysically irreducible to objects)."

25 Perhaps more kindly (professionally) put, Brown has noticed there are communicative details in the interstices of **thing** communication that are not gathered into the conceptual signals of language – signals which makes objecthood possible. Better put (according to the footnoter who thought of it): "objecthood is an emergent property of language".

26 viz Merleau-Ponty: "body is a **thing** among **thing**s". We agree that "soma" would have been better than "body" since "body" comes with its sometimes antithesis "mind". And (again we concur) this duality is really quite misleading, materially speaking, that is.

27 Measurement, in particular of silence, the topic of the next section of THE TEXT, remains critically misunderstood. To understand the depths of such misunderstanding, we agree that deep study of the definitions and scholium of Newton's *Principia* and the responses these sections have caused in the intervening

centuries is worth the effort. In particular, reference to concepts such as absolute time, space, place and motion have caused great mental distress to large numbers and is therefore central to the necessary knot which is human assumption about the context in which humanity takes its living.

[28] AKA, "the geometries of language".

<u>material evaluation</u> | <u>"measurement"</u>

Notation || regarding the section
Systemic processes potentiated within affordances
coalesce under nomina measurement.
| identifiers include |

__positionally acquired information
    , always based upon assumptions
    , take for instance a 6 cm length of string
    | assumption | this 6 cm length will be replicable
    , whether measured in Albania or Mexico
__hominid somatic (aLinguistic) assumptions
    , as in affordance
    are those that tend to work
    (in the context in which the hominid group lives)
    Euclidian space, that is a flat universe (flat-earth in
    another era)
    | one such somatic assumption |
    it might not be true (but)
    (it works within the positional context)
    of THE TEXT and is thus a functional fit of animal
    form
    (with its contingent perceptions) to its environment
__it works because hominids are fundamentally **thing**s
    to be a **thing** is to be a relatively stable
    (reiterative/algorithmically enacting)
    set of affordances
    i.e. chemical processes with a built-in optimal range
    of operations
    & structures (limited by the physics of chemistry) to
    maintain that range
__ it works because the optimal range of perceptual
    operations includes
    , elicitation of feelings (iterations)
    , sensations of value and/or meaning (enactments)
    , feelings/sensations inherent in the relationship
    between **thing**s (**thing**s-in-relation)

___elicitation is part of systemic process
| inscription-edit | 2nd order feedback loop | self-in-relation |

[1] Affordance [here defined]: the act of measuring the world by how well it fits the hand (or mouth - depending on one's stage of development). A fuller definition would include the notion that such measurements do not require awareness, since all chemical constructs react to the world they perceive from the (non-conscious) point of view of their own continuity. So "hand" and "mouth" as the terms of choice show a decided bias toward primate forms. The A-C could have used "flagellum", for example, or "pleural spine".

[2] Stanley – a female hominid named Stanley. Goodness. The A-C has lost its mind.

[3] In our collected opinion, definitions, even of absolutes, are not referencing some unobservable causal agent. THE TEXT makes it clear how this effects the act of measurement. However, the following quote from an unpublished work of the authorial construct adds an important nuance to this position. "The state of a **thing** is definitional and therefore it makes no sense to ask whether a **thing** is real anymore than it makes sense to ask if the definition of the word "**thing**" in the OED is real. What makes the OED useful is its ability to act as a coordinate system by which acts of utterance can be measured and shown to have the status of empirical concordance. The virtue of a definition is in its ability to coordinate physical and social forces with the defined "absolute state". In other words, by referencing the "absolute" OED, we can measure a particular linguistic instantiation of "**thing**". Yet no one charges language with intransigence."

4 Referencing: "Prima materia (o transfórmare): *an alchemical essay*". This piece is of particular note to this section of THE TEXT, largely because of the wildly inappropriate "impure", (to coordinate with the work) use of (pseudo)Latin and some**thing** that sounds vaguely Spanish.

5 Language as a term in this text is not equivalent to communication. Language is taken (for these purposes) as an emergent property of communication and includes the property of abstract categorization [simplification] procedure known as syntax. Syntax is a property of the brain's ability to simulate real world situations and simplify them as images (in the referential space known as "the mind") to allow for accurate prediction at as much distance as possible. For example, it is good to be able to yell "look out, there is a lion coming, and she looks really, really mad" long before the skin feels the lion's claws. Language is particularly good in letting one's chums know in a quick and easy manner (from the safe distance of the sturdy tank in which you are traversing the lion's homeland) a manner that doesn't require the rather time consuming task of miming "claw, fang, pain, run", and "LION!", a manner quite a bit more specific that a simple alarm vocalization.

6 Other ways to measure that do not involve conscious thought: one example involves the measurement of light through the "incremental sensitivity" of membranes. Soma, in other words, does not need a clock, a concept of simultaneity, nor even time, in order to measure. It just has to have a system that does **thing**s with well modulated steps, and much of the material world, being well modulated by virtue of physical and chemical law, does exactly that.

7 To clarify: "Affordance" as a term is used with respect to "**thing**s" by Donald A. Norman (1988) in <u>The Design of</u>

Everyday **Thing**s. In THE TEXT he speaks of the "psychology of materials and of **thing**s, the study of affordances of objects." He goes on to say that "when used in this sense, the term *affordance* refers to the perceived and actual properties of the **thing**, primarily those fundamental properties that determine just how the **thing** could possibly be used. A chair affords ("is for") support and, therefore, affords sitting." It is easy enough to accept the term when applied to **thing**s like doors and teacups, but the term was coined in 1977 by Jerome J Gibson and used to define this same kind of relationship between organisms and their environments, specifically as "the opportunities for action provided by a particular object or environment". The radical suggestion is that "meaning" and "value" are perceived in much the same way as "texture" or "colour". [for the footnoters, the jury is still out]

[8] DiSalle, Robert. 1995. "Space-Time Theory as Physical Geometry"". Erkenntnis Vol 42, No. 3 (May, 1995), pp. 317-337.

[9] A "chair" from the point of view of a beaver "is for" dinner. We'd like to point that out because THE TEXT isn't always clear about the radical mutability of meaning and the content of affordances. Nor, in our opinion, does it take a strong enough stance on positionally acquired information.

[10] We would argue that, in some ways, Stanley has become an object for the authorial construct. Naming, for example, "measures" what we know about hominid development, about each species specifically, against the particular place and time (parameters of inscription) of the primate also known as the authorial construct. Whilst it is never possible for a chemical construct to perceive outside its self-referentially constructed nature (that is the inscription-edit cycle of information transfer is the

construct enacting in and with its environment), there is a rather wide range along the vector which is point-of-view. By naming this particular fossilized form (Stanley!) of a long dead ancestral hominid, the A-C has pulled the hominid into the vortex of the A-C's inscription process.

11 While we agree that the interesting problem with **thing**hood (for the living) is the problem of optimal range maintenance, we feel that this should be subdivided into the problem of maintaining non-aware processes (e.g. ph balance in bodily fluids) and necessarily communicative/aware-of-*notself* processes (e.g. social animal empathy and the neurological structures which enable such feelings).

12 We would have thought that any dividing line between aware and unaware functioned rather like certainty in Descartes and Newton or like "absolutes" already discussed. Having said that, it may be that the authorial construct was slyly referencing "randomness" in the upcoming section. If so, then it was mostly unsuccessful.

13 Here our nominal primate returns to the story. Having developed within (and as a result of) the parameters set by DNA, neuronal predispositions, environmental and social conditions, our primate is now a functioning entity, with somatic assumptions firmly embedded in behavioural sets and processual logics with a tiny window for necessarily aware functioning in the immediate moment of choice - what is called an individual. The ongoing inscription and editing of relationship between our primate, its biochemistry and the physics (social and otherwise) of the world, its various systems (aware and not) continually measure the world against the definitions (absolutes) which are its multiple systems and their optimal range maintenance (ORM). The query here, of course, is how to measure (what to choose as an absolute, or the relevant geometry) the effectiveness of the ORM.

[14] It should be noted that "proximity" is a term with complex usage in the A-C's history. For example, in a eponymous poem, the term is defined as "self directive: stand in Spring and, still, face". And there is the unnamed BW who appears to be both friend and mentor. Also, it is unknown if "BW" is human or even a life form. Also of note: the relationship between "proximity" and "positionally acquired information" is less than crystalline.

[15] Why the authorial construct named its Sinoburius fossil Gertrude is unknown, and unfortunately, each footnoter has a different (and, apparently, fixed in some cases) opinion with respect to the conundrum.

[16] Sinoburius lunaris has been referred to (in a private communication) as "cousin". Thus (with the strong disapproval of one footnoter) we would concur that the A-C does act as if this fossilized life form enacts enough of the kinship code to be considered "fictive" kin. We acknowledge that the A-C is offended by the term "fictive", even if it is correct with respect the coordinating "absolute" of the currently predominant anthropological theory. We have agreed to include the A-C's protestation that "fictive" in this context is a "gross act of mismeasurement".

[17] Almost certainly, Stanley had no name for herself, nor for what children she may have had. She had a brain the size of a chimp's and as far as we know, the social-environmental constraints that measured chimp and environment against survival. Naming is as yet unnecessary to the process of meaning inscription. However, we do agree with the A-C that Stanley attributed meaning and was "conscious" (depending on the particular definition utilized). Also, Stanley likely had strong communication skills, as do extant primates, including the one known as "human". This is not to say

Stanley had language. As the A/C playfully (we assume) indicates with mathematical notation: $L \neq C$.

[18] For social mammals, negotiating both power and vulnerability in multiple situations is a prime example of what the authorial construct intends to reference. (Why it didn't just say that irritates this particular footnoter to an uncomfortable degree, because if it had, it could have mentioned neuronal measurement strategies and how some**thing** so apparently unmeasurable as empathy can be coordinated with mirror neuron activity rates.)

[19] [EXCISED FOOTNOTE] {erratum || removed due to the refusal of the footnoter to translate the excised common term of disparagement into professional language}

[20] "It is perhaps misleading for the eTEXT to use the word 'misleading' when modifying the term 'absolute'. The term does need modification: the aLinguistic and postLinguistic historical baggage the word 'absolute' carries is heavily tied up with non-processual and asystemic (dare we say pre-Euclidean morality). However, for the purposes of the geometry in question, 'absolute' does function as an immovable rock, and is thus absolute."

[21] With "autopoeisis" the authorial construct is referencing the work of Maturana & Varela (*Autopoiesis and Cognition*. English version, 1980). The full opening to the quote: an autopoietic machine is a "machine organized (defined as a unity) as a network of processes of production (transformation and destruction) of components which:..." etc. etc. (p.135).

[22] The A-C has referred to this concept as "life, the anti-entropy machine" but must be understood as a joke. That is, while a temporarily stable chemical construct appears

to increase the organization of the universe, according to R. Swenson at least [EXCISED COMMENT] but more of this in following sections.

[23] "How Gertrude measured the world?" The A-C might as well have asked "What's it like to be a trilobite?" But most of us think the question was asked ironically, or at least a question that is meant to have empirical answers that speak of ranges of visual perception and the like. The problem of qualia still consumes much of the literature, but it appears as if the A-C sees most qualia-talk as another act of mismeasurement. In a (non-documented) conversation between the A-C and one of the gathered footnoters, it reportedly said that measuring an entity by its qualia is akin to measuring the spatial volume of an unplugged toaster by referring to the area its heat occupies when working.

[24] Max Planck (from *Treatise on Thermodynamics* (1903), tr. Alexander Ogg. Longmans, Green: London. §133, p.100): *"Every physical or chemical process in nature takes place in such a way as to increase the sum of the entropies of all the bodies taking any part in the process. In the limit, i.e. for reversible processes, the sum of the entropies remains unchanged.* This is the most general statement of the second law of Thermodynamics." (emphasis in original)

[25] This is a question of measurement. The equation: $\Delta S_{total} = \Delta S_{univ} = \Delta S_{sys} + \Delta S_{surr} > 0$. But how to apply it when entropy is taken to mean chaotic? We do not feel this has been dealt with adequately.

[26] Given the A-C's known temper with respect to door-to-door answer-mongers, it is assumed that this comment on "true morality" was meant as a rebuke.

27 The passage in question: "the *question of whether* arises / only in the judgment of angles / and how many shouldered / degrees / this way or that will result / in the blossom of muscular red-waves, / also known as_____pleasure."

28 The full quote:"(Euclidean geometry) is a formalized way of recognizing one kind of phenomenon (the comparison of freely-movable rigid bodies) as a tool for determining the objective relations among other phenomena (angles and distances between given objects)."

29 The assembled footnoters agree (as, according to one of us, does the authorial construct) that the A-C is vague on causation. However, since, for the purposes of measurement, and the idea that the processes which instantiate various forms of life are largely acts of measurement, we feel that this lack of clarity with respect to causation is moot, since it isn't necessary to the explanation - rather like the concept "god" in the theory of evolution, or the "reality" of "Absolute Space" versus the definition of "Absolute Space" in Newton's *Principia*.

30 Refers to: "(self) as algorithm". In particular the opening line: "Newton rules *prosthetic co-evolution*".

31 We think it better to phrase it thus: Measure | ephemera + eternity.

32 The eTEXT (sometimes referred to as the authorial construct, but also sometimes referred to as "the universe") [here defined] is the moment-by-moment encoding (iteration) of a vast array of connections and the systematization of those (enacting) as the ongoing eTEXT.

[33] Note: the eTEXT operates in silence. Note: the eTEXT is a **thing**. Note: the eTEXT is simultaneously an object. Note: eTEXT: **thing**-in-relation.

[34] Silence is multiplicitous in form. Rather like the many kinds of "rigid bodies" in Euclid's geometry. There is the silence of that which is not encoded – not available to chemical units' sensoriums. There is the silence of the myriad details that are encoded as a single experience in those chemical systems that record memory in some form or other. There is the silence of the experience that is unaware (e.g. UV on pale human skin as it drives). There is the silence of an answerless question (e.g. what is the cause of Euclidean Geometry). There is the silence of a meaningless question.

> [This footnoter, being the only one with a sense of humour, has suggested that this footnote should have a footnote. For example the "e" in "eTEXT" here refers primarily to "ephemeral" and only incidentally as "electronic".]

[35] In other words, what DiSalle is saying is that space-time theory is physical geometry. By this he means that there is a system of rule, relationship, law which is only meaningful in the sense that it is used as a measuring device against the material processes of the ongoing universe. Euclidean geometry, for example is a physical geometry that is a coded set of relationships that make predictions about how **thing**s will be in the world. It predicts, for example, the length of a line given the relationship between the other 2 lines in a right-angled triangle. So if two roads meet at a 90 angle then the slanting road that joins them will have a predictable length. That length will be the same in Tunisia as it is in Oklahoma. This (of course) would not be true in some non-Euclidean geometries.

[36] Language is a social geometry in this sense.

37 One of the footnoters had the experience of a school teacher handing THE TEXT[A] a flat wooden ruler and demanding an accurate measurement of the schoolroom's geodesic representation of the earthly body. This is a stellar example of the assumptions that roam beneath any act of measurement. The teacher's purpose was intended to elicit student outrage, and thus provide an opportunity to open discourse upon the topic of the nature of "absolute" when only definition for the purposes of empirical measurement was intended. It was in this way that this particular footnoter was introduced to Newton's *Principia*. What purpose does this serve the reader of this text? The assembled footnoters have agreed that the authorial construct may have undergone a similar experience and that this may be the generative impulse for this section's original inscription.

A "THE TEXT" here is interchangeable with "eTEXT".

38 Silence: [here defined] as the sound made by chemical and subatomic processes. In the Silence of the universe, material (whether chemical or physical) law is the structure of Silence. It appears as if the authorial construct understands silence as matter's geometry. This idea is expanded upon, to some degree, in other areas of this text, as the diligent reader will note. However, in letters between this footnoter and the construct (private communication), it is clear that this idea of silence is best exemplified through the A-C's choice of locations for reading Newton, Euclid and related materials.

39 Clearly both "dictionology" and "diplumyin" are, in most of the footnoters' opinions, made up words. In one footnoter's opinion they qualify as neologisms.

40 In this text "systemic processes" refers generally to 2nd order systems theory. This will be more carefully developed in later chapters, but we appreciate the

inclusion early in this text since it is a subject prone to tendentious constructs. As an exemplar, we refer readers back to footnote 19 in this section.

[41] The full quote (DiSalle, 1995): "To claim that space is Euclidean *only means* that measurements agree with the Euclidean metric; Euclidean geometry, if true, can't *causally explain* those measurements, because it only expresses the constraints to which those measurements will conform....To claim that the formal structure is *really* the structure of actual space is not to posit an underlying cause of the appearances. It is only to claim that, *modulo* the initial coordination, the appearances conform to the laws of that structure. This claim is no less a form of realism than the supposed causal postulate. But it is a form of realism that captures much more clearly the relationship between geometry and experience." (Emphasis in original.)

[42] Referencing: "How the summer rain married your bamboo", in particular "Still, by the time gowns unhung / themselves and paraded, / the bamboo was hugely pregnant / and all of us got caught in / birth's deluge".

<u>material evaluation</u> | <u>"randomness"</u>

Notation || regarding the section
Self (& self-in-relation) constructs, in particular linguistic constructs, impose nomina on processes in order to reduce apparent chaos. | identifiers include |

___mist-rise and i fins on, leaving me to follow imaginary
    anglerfish, its caudle fin flash; peduncle flex;
___bobbing bioluminescent esca, hanging as it does from
    a modified dorsal spine, the illicium, and i jumps
    illicit illuminate
___ illmenium illure illuminati...jaw open for dictive flash,
    snitch snatch & i looks back, imagines its own small
    light as the universe peering___imagines its
    tethering body as impediment

1 We concur (and are still sniggering). What the A-C meant was simply that meaninglessness for human beings is meaningless, and all that is really happening is a movement from Euclidean to Geodesic social geometries making old measurement systems less than illuminating.

2 The pronoun "me" in this case is used to reference soma or the fish's body exclusive of its colony of bioluminescent bacteria.

3 Llinás also defines self: "the generated abstraction called "self" is fundamentally no different from these secondary qualities of the senses; self is the invention of an intrinsic CNS semantic. It exists inside the closed system of the CNS as an attractor, a vortex without true existence other than as the common impetus of otherwise unrelated parts" (p.128). The A-C apparently considers this support for its notion that self = the colour blue (colour being one of those "secondary qualities", although it does acknowledge that multiple selves-in-relation surfacing from the relatively stable chemical construct of soma-

moving-in-the-world (**thing**-in-relation), is perhaps not what Llinás was talking about in that section of the <u>Vortex</u> text.

[4] We prefer an example used in an earlier version of this text: "To complain that sudden darkness is evidence of the cessation of the universe is akin to the lantern fish panicking like Chicken Little. If the fish's colony of bioluminescent bacteria suddenly left the dangling "lantern" the fish uses to attract prey, then it might be hungry for a bit, but such darkness does not signal universal cessation. It is unlikely that deep water neighbours will notice any change whatsoever."

[5] Random [here defined]: $F^{-1}(B) = \{\omega \in \Omega | F(\omega) \cap B \neq \emptyset\} \in F\}$. Exactly.

[6] Random $\neq$ Chance.

[7] Borel's Law does not say that improbable **thing**s do not happen. It says $\underline{\frac{X_n(E)}{n}} \to p$ as $n \to \infty$.

[8] We recommend a delightful hour with http://rationalwiki.org/ where it shows (using Littlewood's Law) that some miracles (defined as "any unlikely event") have a 63.2% chance of occuring.

[9] Probability is analytical in nature, not autopoeitic. Probability analyszes random phenomena; it is not identical with the phenomena it analyzes.

[10] Perhaps this footnote is unneccessary for the discerning reader, but the origins of symbolic systems (incl. language) and their "purpose" remain highly contentious.

11 The A-C is signalling its coordinating absolute with respect to language. Phrases such as "to grow our conceptual reach, so that we can reach a bit further past our own animal needs" implies an understanding of social/environmental processes as selecting for those social animals that can more fully embody the Other for the purposes of social coordination. Please refer to future sections of this text on inter-kingdom signalling for a more complete discussion.

12 Kinship [here defined]: "a kind of randomness that feels meaningful". The "Cute Response" (viz *Kindchenschema*, Conrad Lorenz, 1943) is an example that might have been salient in this section.

13 "Encoded empathy" here references mirror neurons enacting in an enviroment where the **thing**-in-relation has noticed the existence of the Other.

14 "Randomness" in this section refers to planetary processes as they affect the rise and fall of relatively stable chemical constructs. In other words, massive planetary changes such as the poisoning of the atmosphere with cyanobacteria O_2 farts (if they had anuses), caused (~2.4 billion years ago) "The Great Oxygenation Event" or "The Oxygen Catastrophe" (depending on which side of the death-line you favoured). The end of many kinds of chemical constructs also provided an opportunity for many more. Gertrude Sinebarius lunaris, for example (Life span of trilobites ~521 million years ago ↔ ~250 million years ago). Or the authorial construct itself (Life span of extant AMH *sapiens*, genus *Homo,* tribe *Hominini*) ~200,000 years ago ↔ ~unknown.

15 All the A-C appears to be saying is that language (or symbolic systems in general) make humans really bad at recognizing, or dealing with, randomness - a bit like how

ice has a hard time dealing with heat. This is in part why meaninglessness[B] is meaningless for human beings.

[B] meaniglessness ≠ grief at the loss of presumed privileged

[16] Applicable to Excel: Generate a random real number: RAND()*(b-a)+a. Inapplicable anywhere else.

[17] While it is true that the inbuilt limitations of chemistry affect what can be perceived in stable chemical constructs (aka animals, in this case), it is also true that each animal has a small range of **thing**s (aka other chemical constructs), (not necessarily other animals, nor even living constructs) that afford the animal an opportunity to meet its needs. In other words, it is evolutionarily economical to make (or leave) what doesn't matter to the animal imperceptible.

[18] In this way, language works to make unimportant details dissapear. The problematizing of language (through glossalia, or poetry, as examples) can temporarily make such details "visible". Hence the A-C's interest in "ghosts".

[19] In this way language, while reducing apparent chaos for the localized chemical construct, in fact increases general entropy.

[20] In this way, Silence is spatially articulated.

[21] References "aphasia": "a slug on a salt trail   so you get out because you   know and you ...postinch dur albesto...   ".

[22] This is pure speculation. We cannot know many **thing**s. Certainly not about how Gertrude felt upon her death, not even the exact manner of her death. Based on her anatomy, the environmental conditions of her time, the

kinds of other constructs that occupied the earth, we can perhaps make good educated assumptions about what she ate, what scared her, what drew her attention, what she safely ignored. We can't know the specifics of her individuality, the delightful angular degree at which her tentacles bent when she was satisfied of her hunger, or the degree to which she cocked her legs when she was on the prowl.

23 Silence [here defined] is the aLinguistic world. eTEXT in this context refers to the communicative systems developed through evolution enabling successful information management by relatively stable chemical units and the environs in which those units attempt to sustain genetic/system existence. THE ephemeral TEXT (in the case of human beings) utilizes symbolic encasement of vast, essentially infinite, systemic processes and represents them as a set of movements (the arm extended directly in front of the body with hand held rigidly up toward the sky) or even more succinctly with the word (STOP). But just try to dig into the word "stop" and see how much other material is there. The length of that string is endless and twisted, and is never situationally independent even within a singular "geometry".

24 The role of the placenta with regard to human evolution, in particular the processes necessary to encephalization, is understudied.

25 Patterns and lack thereof in deep time. Euclidean and Geodesic geometries. Linguistic and aLinguistic chemical constructs. "Never forget that Random is a Word, and thus fuctions as an absolute."

26 AKA "embodied cognition". See Wilson, A. D. & Golonka, S. "Embodied cognition is not what you think it is" (2013) Front. Psychol., 12 February 2013 | doi: 10.3389/fpsyg.2013.00058.

²⁷ Lakoff, G. & Johnson, M. (1980). <u>Metaphors We Live By</u>. Chicago: University of Chicago.

²⁸ The footnoters admit to being evolutionary modules. To begin the process of symbolic representation, a life form must be able to manipulate representational material – what human beings call being "aware". In the hominid line (and many, many others), what follows basic awareness is communication. Such strategies are aLinguistic and yet underpin language. Each emergent communication property forms a module, which later enables a further emergent property, which itself becomes a module - AKA **thing**s- or selves-in-relation.

²⁹ We refer readers to material on thalamic organization, R.S. Swenson, <u>Review of Clinical and Functional Neuroscience</u>, for example. It is important to understand that the modular approach is only functional because of the organizing nature of other areas of the brain. This involves individual (cells) giving up certain "powers" to enable the whole (organism) to function in a motile environment. This is the very basis of multicellular life. Later, the A-C will argue that the same strategy is at work in the development of functional society.

³⁰ What has been ignored here: between melodies and modules there is silence. We agree that this is an important concept and should have been directly discussed in THE TEXT.

³¹ Referencing "between melodies": "presses inward toward breaking, / cows begin to run & bellow, the cats / unleash, dogs prepare for war".

³² According to THE TEXT, we are **thing**s-in-relation. As far as **thing** theory goes, the eTEXT is a **thing** in the sense that it is a generalized a-specific object – or cluster of a-specific objects. A **thing** is a material representation of a

set of processes. (In this way a **thing** is like a word, and *vice versa*.) In all cases, **thing**s are **thing**s-in-relation.

33 Yes. It was some random act that meant it was Gerturde's form that survived as a fossil, as it will be some 260 million years from now if it is that particular hominid mentioned in THE TEXT whose brain case is replaced by mineral and glows brownly because of that far future sun. All the other hominids (not caught in the random act) will just be particulate in whatever constitutes the new dominant species' "morning tea".

34 For clarification purposes, an alternative example from an earlier text: "A **thing** is a material concept. Just as the linguistic concept "apple" is a generalized **thing** (contra object viz Brown) that encapsulates, and attempts to still, a constantly morphing system of processes, a sensible (or material) **thing** in the world like a human body is just such an attempt – to maintain a constantly morphing set of chemical processes and keep them in stasis…We know that the singularity and apparent certainty of the material concept "body" is incorrect because a human body sheds itself. Is the sloughed skin the I? It is if you're a murderer and you get caught because some tech found your skin cells on the corpse of your victim. It's not if it has become part of some other human that ate the fruit that took in the nitrates sloughed off in the decomposition of cells you lost 20 years ago…Still, the (material) concept (of "**thing**" or "I" or "self") works to reduce the chaos that would ensue if animals had to think of themselves as schmeared out over the world as they in fact are…So "I" is a useful conceptual tool, both materially and linguistically."

35 Silence is in no way able to be legitimately (viz DiSalle) coordinated with randomness. For that matter, there is no algorithmically stable relationship between silence and entropy. (In this sense they equal no**thing**, or more specifically they do not equal Ø.)

[36] The difference is contingency and consequence.

[37] Referencing "carrion flowers": "For now, we are just this: / no flowers, instead, chemistry ravenous for home."

[38] We disagree with this. It seems far more likely that the inclusion of random events in the sustainability of particular life forms in the ongoing processes of natural selection make it likely that the bricolage nature of communication systems is sensed as a seamless whole due to energy constraints. In the assembled footnoters opinion, it seems far too neurologically expensive to maintain awareness of the discrete communicative (not to mention linguistic) processes. The definitive loss of information that comes with the illusion of a seamless whole is manifestly less costly since human life forms appear quite successful in populating their environments.

[39] The original line read (with formatting intact):
"Deleuze said that Leibniz implies that if god
is $\frac{\infty}{1}$
then the individual notion
is $\frac{1}{\infty}$ "

[40] The equation would read: Silence (R^0) = {$\infty \in 1 | R(0) \cap R\ 1 \in \infty$ }

[41] The proposition: Stanley is aLinguistic and Stanley can think. Since we know there are aLinguistic, thinking humans today, this seems a reasonable line of inquiry.

[42] Reference: "**Thing** Theory and the predisposition of apples to be eaten by worms".

[43] The current iteration of the quote: "Whether we see and interact with the elements of material reality (as made

available to us through our sensorium) as **thing**s or as objects is a matter of our particular animal needs. All self-sustaining chemical systems have mechanisms by which the desirable is sought and the undesirable is avoided. Humans can code this in a variety of ways, but one common coding is as "good" and "bad". Often such mechanisms are known as "feelings" despite their chemical origins." [originating text - in press]

44 References: "creative longing and the number line" (viz "irrationals are dangerous").

45 [1/ "Certainty", first and foremost, is a word.] [2/ So is "metaphor".] [3/ Humans are not lantern fish.] [4/ Humans are no longer Australopithecines.] In our gathered opinion the first two are obvious and the last two make no sense. Hence, we advised the A-C to omit. It ignored us.

46 Keywords: randomness [link 404]; illusory correlation [link 404]; judgment biases [link 404]; rational analysis [link 404]; Bayesian inference [link 404].

47 The "Law of Large Numbers" is a part of probability theory that says that with a great many trials the average of the results will be close to the expected value. This applies to evolution (future section) in the sense that random mutations are the equivalent of trials. The enormous number of generations already accomplished by chemical constructs represent billions and billions of "trials".

48 Our primate, now on the road to placental development, a process which enables encephalization, which in turn, enables symbolic systems and conceptual autopoiesis.

49 Random ≠ meaningless. "In fact, apart from TheGeometryOfFeeling, these terms are representative of quite different geometries" (private communication).

<u>material evaluation</u> | <u>"evolution"</u>

Notation || regarding the section
Identity position coalesces under conditions of deep time
| identifiers include |

___kinship between kingdoms
    , on fossils, rabbits, early hominids, and earthworms
    , upper paleolithic figurines
    , the domestication of humans by roses
___signal amplification
    and the distinction between communicative and
    linguistic code modification | distinction resting
    upon
    , the somatic symphony with choral sections
    [acoustic] intact
    , the tin whistle of language [amplified]
    , the odd case of cognitively normal a-Linguistic
    adult humans
___codification (resulting)
    exemplar of the consequences of signal amplification
    in social primates
    , **thing**s versus objects
    , nevertheless resting upon strategies persistent in
    bacterial life forms
    , AKA inter-kingdom signalling

[1] While this research initially coordinates within bacterial populations and studies signalling between bacterial cells of the same population, it has become clear that signalling practices exist between bacterial colonies and their hosts. Since "it is estimated that humans have 10^{13} human cells and 10^{14} bacterial cells", this ability of bacterial cells to communicate (e.g. coordinate cellular activity) is germane to the current discussion of the role language plays in aiding the emergence of human community.

[2] Arguments regarding reproduction versus metabolism as the master code have made the literature interesting of late. In particular, it appears as if the A-C takes particular pleasure in arguments about the causal nature of each with respect to hominid encephalization. It has been known to call these "the placental wars". Partly, we assume, this is because of the problem of maternal and embryonic competition over scarce resources and the role this must have played in the nutritional cost of carrying an embryo that needs dense nutritional resources to grow a big brain. However, there may be an element of awareness in the A-C (in its naming) of the academic gender wars, and human (researcher or not) predispositions to see through one's own glass.

[3] Self [here defined] as situationally partinent (contingent) evolutionary modules. These modules (e.g. the skin self, osteo self, eye self, vestibular self, etc.) are coralled by the thalamus to present a simplified predictive model of the external world. (The predictive function explains contingency). It remains possible, with conscious attention, to listen to the skin self, the eye self, etc.

[4] Llinás (2002, p.50) *"The brain's control of organized movement gave birth to the generation and nature of the mind"* (emphasis in original). Also, "Blueness is a brain interpretation given to a particular wavelength (420 nm) range" (p. 100).

[5] We concur. Bacteria are the living epitome of the power of silence.

[6] The tin whistle was explained this way (private communication): "Imagine you are at a production of Beethoven's 9th symphony. There they are. All the musicians, the singers, the instruments, the chairs, stands, passive acoustic manangement devices. This is

"communication". This is the wonderful evolutionary history of soma, of the eTEXT. It reads and is read. It listens and plays. Then a little kid comes along with a tin whistle. This is language. Here's what makes it so overwhelimg - the tin whistle is amplified. It blows B's audience (i.e. their awareness) out of the concert hall. Not that the musicians stop playing, but attention is diverted. The tin whistle has them all agog. Even if the kid has (currently) a really tiny repetoire. Because of the tin whistle and its amplifiers, it takes real work to listen to the 9th."

7 Language can be considered an emergent property of silence in this same way.

8 Natural selection aka "the engine of evolution" rests upon the imprecision of sexual reproduction with respect to the faithful copying of genetic material. This imprecision is known as "mutation". Mutation is random in the sense that it is an error which is not predictable.

9 Of the suggestion, that by this time in hominid development, hominid groups must have begun showing signs of linguistic behaviour is still speculative. However, the obligate nature of extant primate vocalizations (including many human ones) does suggest that vocal languages were secondary to manual ones. Hence a signing *Homo* can stand until further research suggests otherwise.

10 Bonner, J. T. (2013). *Randomness in Evolution.* Princeton University Press.

11 We recommend further study. Suggestions include: "Hughes, D. T. & Sperandio V. (2008). "Inter-kingdom signalling: communication between bacteria and their hosts". *Nature Reviews Microbiology* V. 6, pp.111-120; Pacheco, A.R. & Sperandio, V. (2009). Inter-kingdom

signaling: chemical language between bacteria and host. *Current Opinion in Microbiology*. V.12, pp.192-198.

[12] We repeat: random ≠ chance.

[13] Erratum: The article title was in fact "Predictable Evolution Trumps Randomness of Mutations" as printed in the cited issue of <u>Scientific American</u>.

[14] Gertrude Trilobyte and sea squirts that eat their own brains. We concur that THE TEXT is inadequate with respect to the connection between these two forms of stable chemical constructs. The fact that sea squirts bud their young with enough brain matter to make their short-lived mobility viable, and then, once rooted, digest their own (now useless) brains seems no**thing** at all like what is known about Gertrude's life style choices. Afterall she remained mobile from birth until death. She needed her brain to manage all those left-right-up-down decisions that had to be made quickly and accurately. One footnoter has suggested that it is just sour-grapes on the part of the A-C—that Gertrude and her kin are (mostly) dead and sea squirts are doing fine. There might be some**thing** in that given the following (inappropriate) textual commentary on the political intelligence of hominids.

[15] To clarify, most mutations are of no consequence. That is, the vast majority of transcription errors make no practicable difference to the functioning of the organism. Some, however are "bad" (to accord with the moral terminology used by the A-C). This simply means the organism has a distinct disadvantage. Some are "good". This means the organism has a distinct advantage.

[16] The archaeological argument referred to here is often known as the "Home Base-Food Sharing" model. See Domínguez-Rodrigo and Pickering for further details.

[17] With no intention of seeming ridiculous, we question these questions: "Is 'evolution' a **thing**?" & "Is [evolution] silent?"

[18] Mutational advantage only signifies if the "good" trait is passed on to future generations. This means 1) it must be inheritable and 2) the organism must have offspring that also have offspring. Needless (perhaps) to say the organisms unlucky enough to have a "bad" mutation often don't have offspring that survive. In this way the "good" mutations become common.

[19] Referencing: "bull in love" | in particular "her tail on the fly-sprung wind"

[20] For example: "At the transition to *Homo* someone comes up with a unique way to signal "go left". The unique quality is its replicability. The specific hand gesture means. And it means regardless of situation or signer. This is communication transgressing onto linguistic territory. The hand gesture is a sign. The gesture now has transferable content. This is what makes it a sign. We imagine such a "mutation" turned out to be terribly useful when stealing a dead ibex from a family of lions" (in press).

[21] Encephalization is an example of a "good" mutation. Although we encouraged the A-C to omit such a paticularly laden (moral) term, it persisted in this (from our perspective) error.

[22] Gilbert, M. T. P., et.al. (2008). "DNA from Pre-Clovis Human Coprolites in Oregon, North America" *Science* V.320, pp.786-789.

[23] Excised.

[24] The irritant? The set of assumptions that underlies the phrase "Man the hunter." The A-C's footnote has been excised. We find this unfortunate, but neverless necessary.

[25] Stenzel, D. & Huttner, W.B. (2013) "Role of maternal thyroid hormones in the developing neocortex and during human evolution." Max Planck Institute of Molecular Biology and Genetics, Dresden, Germany.

[26] The pertinent footnote for the poem "Origins" reads: "In May of 1792 George Vancouver's ship "Discovery" gets laid on its side by low tide, and in his spinning ire, he names the place Useless Bay." Naming. Exactly. Self-in-relation.

[27] The full quote: Stenzel & Huttner (2013) "Hominid evolution, which is characterized by increased cognitive skills and abilities due to the drastically enlarged neocortex, has been linked to iodine availability...it is not so much the genetic regulation and alteration in gene expression by thyroid hormones that resulted in the evolutionary expansion of the brain, but much more the tweaking of thyroid hormones in a dose- and time-dependent fashion and thereby exhibiting different effects on different brain regions that enable the increase in cognitive abilities."

[28] Brains are expensive. It is for this reason that bioenergetics and the study of the archaeological evidence for brain expansion, especially around 1.8 million years ago [viz *Homo erectus*] is critical support for the A-C's notion as presented here.

[29] Referencing: "& we, audience to the low-toned concerto / here at the coffee shop, espresso outside in limpid winter, / at tables clustered with spoons, / elbows and

knees poke holes in thin-skinned air; / we carry on mumbling."

30 As a matter of brain-to-body weight comparison: *Homo sapiens*»2.28 | *Pan troglodytes*»0.80 | *Orcinus orca*»0.26 | *Delphinus delphis*»1.35.

31 We find it odd that for the A-C, Gertrude and her ancient passing leads to such grief. We do understand the A-C's obsession with deep time, but Gerturde didn't even know about the possibility of the A-C. It makes no sense. The A-C's response to a polite inquiry re this emotional anomaly? "And really, how can an emotional distinction be made between the death of the triolobytes and the imminent passing of lions and tigers and bears? Should I not feel sad for that?"

32 Referencing: "Is the Buddha Still Showing Up in the Pope's Morning Toast"

33 Why a tin whistle?

34 This footnoter would speak on behalf of the A-C by pointing out that "Stanley" is variously *Australopithecine*, *Homo erectus* and occasionally *habilis*. We suggest that Stanley remains most fully in the field of **thing**s because of the "floating" name-identity. It is more that that A-C has objectified its own past rather than the specific fossilized hominids unlucky enough to have been caught by sudden burial.

35 Marino, L. (1998). "A Comparison of Encephalization between Odontocete Cetaceans and Anthropoid Primates". *Brain, Behavior and Evolution*. V.51, pp.230-238.

36 Are there descendents of Gertrude? We cannot know if Gertrude produced young. But given current

understanding of the tree of evolutionary life, no. Gertrude and her kind are considered extinct. However there are extant arthropods—Gertrude's cousins if you will: Chelicerates (spiders, scorpions); Myriapods (centipedes); Crustaceans (shrimp, crabs, lobsters); Hexapods (insects).

[37] In fact Marino ranks H. sapiens, S. fluviatilis, L. obliquidens, D. delphis and T. truncatus in the first category with regard to encephalization quotient.

[38] Schaller, Susan (1995). *A Man Without Words*. University of California Press.

[39] Notes, but we assembled here on this 2-D world (page or screen) consider it much more ironic that the extension of self which language allows, and the wonderful integration that words allow with respect to the environment (**thing**s-in-relation / selves-in relation) is also a large part of the reason we feel so isolated.

<u>material evaluation</u> | <u>"consciousness"</u>

Notation || regarding the section
Consciousness coalesces under conditions of an evolutionary impetus to measure time through muscular control. | identifiers include |

___the blue waters of a deep sigh
___the lightning strike of expectation
___the breaking breath of morning light
___the muscular curve of cool evening air
___the smooth bend of a folding sunset
___the silky pouch of noon's shade
___the gut rumble of moon rise
___the clench and release of running water

[1] "When your toaster dies, where does the heat go?" (from the unpublished ephemera of the authorial construct).

[2] In an unpublished account, the A-C has also described this phenomenon thusly: "Imagine you are on a dark mountainside. You leave the cabin to walk to the outhouse. Using your flashlight you get halfway there and realize, that apart from the small ball of yellow light centered on the pathway, you cannot see any**thing** else. You flash the light toward the sound coming from the underbrush up the slope to your right, but the light is too weak to make any**thing** out at that distance. In other words, the light is such that it has a very short range of usefulness for such a big world. And in some ways it is acutely dangerous. After all, you can't see whatever it is rummaging around in the brush, but with that light, every**thing** on the mountain can see you. So you turn off the light for a while. It takes time, but after a few minutes of what seems to you as utter dark, your senses adjust. And you can see, hear, sense well enough to make your way to the outhouse door. What you won't see: if the jackass from earlier in the day left the seat down when he-

missed-the-hole-so-you-have-to-clean-it-up-before-you-sit-down. For that kind of the **thing**, the flashlight is really useful."

3 What this case study proves most simply is that consciousness and language are not identical. More importantly, it establishes that rational thought, the capacity to apply logic to material problems, is also independent of language.

4 Consciousness [here defined]: an absolute against which social primates measure evolutionary potential in self and other. (Please refer back to fn 3 in the section on measurement for clarifaction of intent.)

5 Back to the question of what Gertrude thought about! THE TEXT suggests that awareness is a necessary attribute of self-referentially mobile life forms. Decisions have to be made about left or right and those decisions require thought if they are to be reactions to unique circumstances. They might be simple thoughts, or perhaps feelings would be a better term in English. So where an extant hominid might "think" *Tiger to the left, run right* (probably slightly later than the flight reflex enacts), Gertrude might have "felt" *AAAAAAARGH IMMINENT PAIN APPROACHING RUN AWAY FROM FEAR*. Feelings, here-in, are somatic thoughts. Feelings are material concepts that are utilized by chemical constructs to transmit information and instruction to muscular groupings and generate appropriate fixed behavioural responses. Feelings are a proven way (in animal life in particular) to get **thing**s done. "I WANT" whether in (reasoned) words of wordless (longing) is a powerful motivator of hand-eye or tentacle-tooth coordination, and to be blunt, feelings are far more powerful a motivator in extant hominids than any**thing** approaching rationality. So we concur. Gertrude felt a lot about **thing**s like food, mating, ocean temperature, the

presence of light, certain types of movement, etc. She can be said to be aware in the sense that she likely tracked all these **thing**s. But she had no self – because "self" or ("I") as we are using the term in this context refers to that construct created by the thalamocortical assemblage to manage the needs of a completely different set of construct-envrionmental parameters. Gertrude didn't need this kind of "I" so she wouldn't have gone to the evolutionary expense of building one. She was no sea squirt.

6 Monod, J. (1971). <u>Chance and Necessity: an Essay on Natural Philosophy of Modern Biology</u>. New York: Alfred A. Knopf.

7 Defined as the inappropriate reading of human ways onto non-human beings, "anthropomorphism" signifies a limited point of view and a probable lack of respect for non-self entities. Unless, of course, the perpetrator is a very young child, or otherwise a human entity incapable of Otherhood recognition.

8 The footnoters mostly agree. Causal theories (of consciousness) may be relegated to the same pile as causal theories of Euclidean geometry.

9 Consciousness [here defined] is the act of measurement coordinated with the geometry of chemical structure's communicative systemics.

10 Consciousness [here {also} defined] is both the little wooden ruler and the 6 cm line. It is an emergent property of a chemical construct needing to coordinate multiple movements in multiple rapidly occuring circumstances within a organically defined Euclidean space/geometry.

11 Consciousness [defined by another construct] "a noncontinuous event determind by simultaneity of

activity in the thalamocortical system" (Llinás and Pare 1991). In the 2002 text: "Global temporal mapping generates cognition."

[12] Evolutionary potential may lay in the inclusion of the geodesic in conscious systemics.

[13] If consciousness is an evolutionarily emergent tool, it may well act as an "opposable thumb" in the field of the conceptual. If so, then the possibility of "reaching beyond" soma's point of view may be possible for some future hominid.

[14] Like looking in your sideview mirror and seeing a train rushing away.

[15] It is also possible that consciousness is just another sensory organ (akin to the vestibular) that allows us to reduce the confusion inherent in a complex social world. If the confusion can be reduced to manageable bits of information through categorization and labelling, evolutionary potential is likely enhanced.

[16] Llinás, R.R. (2002). I of the vortex: from Neurons to Self. Cambridge, Massachusetts: MIT Press.

[17] It is a delightful irony (as the A-C pointed out) that the apparent increase in order gained by the onset of language is accompanied by a general increase in social entropy. However, we (footnoters) all agree that using the "Facebook Time Sink" is a tad facetious as an exemplar of an otherwise serious subject.

[18] The question "what is it like to be a cognitively normal adult human being with no language" is a good one. We do wish the A-C had answered it more thoroughly. The reference to repetitive gesturing, ritual enactments and the creation of event specific (i.e. non-generalizable)

gestures of memory and meaning are well enough, but for this language user (in particular) it is not enough.

19 The full quote: "Imagine that every time you wanted to get an apple from someone you had to go through the entire physical story—a shared memory of going to pick an apple from a tree. Imagine that you couldn't sign or say "apple" or gesture "want". Painful enough, but what if you had no shared history on which to mime the actions of going to go pick an apple. How would you communicate this need to a stranger? This is what generalizable signs make possible. This is the power of language. I can talk to people I don't know. To then refuse the Other because of fear, how utterly ridiculous." (in press)

20 Our primate Stanley and her near descendants aside for a moment, the more salient question would be what is it like to think about the world and about self without langauge. That it is possible is clear. And that the acquisition of language drastically shifts the nature of primate thinking is also clear. But it seems uncontrovertible that the (reiterative, recursive, gestural, behavioural) communicative foundation upon which language rests doesn't vanish in the moment the power of external, arbitrary conceptual frames (aka language) are realized by "the mind".

21 Monod: "implies the idea of an oriented, coherent, and constructive activity" —this describes "teleonomy". Compare this to the concept of "affordance".

22 Like any definition of "life", the term "consciousness" is not terribly definitive. As with life, we know conscious when we see it. Which of course is really quite funny because we often don't, not even with our own kind. For example take the fear that one would be taken for dead by the world and buried alive—for those with the funds, the practice of giving the "corpse" a bell-pull just in case was

at its height during the 18th and 19th centuries. In other places, Munich for example, set up "waiting mortuaries" where families (for a fee) could bring their dead and await putrefaction - just to be sure before the dead relation was put in the ground. (We understand the A-C considered using this in THE TEXT, but since it didn't we thought to properly include it here.) [See: Bondenson 1997, Jan. <u>A Cabinet of Medical Curiosities.</u> London: I. B. Tauris for further details.]

[23] "The tin whistle and its oscillations": referencing an organism's neurologically based problem of organizing movement. Llinás links coordinated neuronal groups (i.e. communication between groups of neurons) through in-phase oscillation. His work aims to show how coordinated activity is the neurological root of consciousness. Note how reminiscent this "in-phase" neuronal activity is to inter-kingdom signalling (quorum sensing across Kingdom boundaries) of bacteria and their hosts.

[24] To a large extent, what Llinás is calling "prosody" the A-C is calling communication.

[25] Social encephalization [here defined] the growth and increased speed of information networks in society that enable better predictive ability to the society as a whole, and (importantly) links accurate prediction to appropriate action networks.

[26] Keyword: prediction. Might explain the A-C's fascination with magical systems.

[27] "By these standards proteins must be deemed the essential molecular agents of teleonomic performance in living beings" (p. 45). Monod.

28 Silence [here defined] is the condition of not having the perceptual ability to perceive the inscription/edit/inscription systemic cycle.

29 In Llinás, the senses are modules that are linked into a perceptual whole by the thalamocortical system.

30 "The thalamocortical system constitutes the vast majority of the mammalian brain, and increases disproportionately (allometrically) with overall brain size" (Granger, R.H. and Hearn R. A. (2007). Scholarpedia 2(11): 1796 doi:10.4249/scholarpedia.1796.

31 No longer a long string of data from the environment/organism interface, nor left to soma for a flight or fight response, consciousness [here {contextually} defined] is a turn sign and a set of traffic lights when there are multiple ways to go.

32 Would such an expensive evolutionary tool be necessary except in certain circumstances? Like encephalization generally, there must have been some payoff for the evolving creatures. So it seems to us an unnecessary question given the ground work already laid.

33 The **thing** about consciousness, is that it is not dependent upon language, but communication. However, as the case of Ildefonso (*A Man Without Words*) shows, language recrystalizes consciousness. It is probably very much like a lantern fish that gains a bioluminescent community and thus is far less hungry most of the time. The price it pays: it can no longer see the sea.

34 With a lovely sense of humour Llinás says "The brain is quite Kantian in the essence of its operation." He goes on to say that "It makes representations of aspects of the external world, fractionalized aspects, by making a useful geometry, a geometry with internal meaning that has

no**thing** to do with the "geometry" of the external world that gave rise to it." We understand from one of us that the A-C was drinking grape juice at this specific time of reading (viz Kant) and that the shirt is now permanently stained from the resulting laughter, which in turn resulted in a nasally expectorated purple fluid. Further, the A-C has said this is a good example of emergent structures (referring to the shirt) and properties (referring to the unintended behaviour) as a result of material (incl. language) interaction (personal communication).

[35] "The monkey-mind is the price we pay for language." We concur that this assertion lacks evidentiary support.

[36] Better put, "using language to disrupt language enables we primates to "hear" the body". Still we concur that it is bloody hard conceptual work and therefore unlikely to pertain to the vast majority of extant hominids. (private communication)

Notation || regarding the section
Silence coalesces under the condition of ineptitude in the field of objects. | identifiers include |

___OBJECT | the bioluminescent bacterial community whinging about the stalking fish
___OBJECT | the chemical construct (hominid) bemoaning the needs of others (human and not)
___OBJECT | the skin-self complaining about the osteo-self
___OBJECT | the night complaining about the demands of the day
___OBJECT | the heat over the toaster bemoaning the closeness of the cold (from its point of view) metal
___OBJECT | the linguistic-self whinging about the stalking silence

[1] Silence and its relationship to **things**? We believe that the A-C is suggesting that to think of oneself as a **thing** (i.e. a generalizable part of a field of **things**) is to come closer to thinking systemically than is possible with the speech of objects.

[2] From "Hermes descending a staircase". The particular lines in question are: & winged heels | diamonds dropped shatter / under foot | curve of calf muscling apart identity / & snakes come loose | the restraining staff, / the wo | the we | the man, and the message comes / tumbling

[3] In other words, to become an object is to gain specificity and to remove oneself at least one step from the system which is only partly "self". It is like the lantern fish placing its identity in the lantern with it bioluminescent colony of bacteria. To do so is to ignore the necessary fish with it modified dorsal spine which hangs the lantern in the deep. It is also to ignore the teeth and the evoloutionary

consequence of the lantern – that is, of course, to eat well enough to keep going. To think of oneself as a **thing** is to move "self" back to include the fish, its teeth, the bacteria, the lantern and the spine. Silence would be to include all those **thing**s plus the surrounding sea. Self becomes meaningless at this point, and thus becomes silent in the larger Silence. Again: self / self-in-relation; **thing** / **thing**-in-relation.

4 It should be noted that (contra one particular of we footnoters) that the language-self has a particularly bad habit of relegating non-linguistic selves to a "sub" self level with regard to the overall system/construct.

5 Silence is that identity locator one step beyond **thing**. It is the position of self immolation, and conceptual reunification with the system.

6 From "Indian apocalypse". Please reference the 2nd section which reads (with formatting intact):

> fall fields, green hint of winter's crop
> clouds in broken columns vault
> flashing by
> but still
> goshawk waits

7 Noise, then, reflects the idea of the roaring conflict between disparate affordances. The "self of the skin" has one set of "logics" by which the external world is assessed. The "self of the vestibular" has another. All perceptual organs have affordances which enable their part of the system to keep operating within acceptable limits. Just like sodium pumps and electron ladders in the functioning of cells, each has its own construct to maintain. Each is a self-in-relation.

8 Language is the noisiest self humans have. It has its own set of affordances.

9 From another work of the A-C: "Language creates the field of objects - or at least the field of objects is an emergent property of language which, in its turn, emerged from the somatic capacity for abstract thought in communication" (unpublished).

10 The underlying text is the-moment-of-the-body-thinking-through-the-relationship-to-a-fossilized-trilobite, taken for kin the long-dead and the never-living.

11 Language = the amplified tin whistle.

12 Gertrude is now silently sitting on some primate neck. If she was silent during the mobile years as a non-fossilized chemical construct is unknown. It is likely that her legs made sounds as they moved around under the sea, but that these sounds would have had limited perceptibility to Gertrude because sound in the water is not often a primary sensory guidance system. So "Silence" wouldn't have the been the code word for her longing to exceed her limitations. Given the usefulness of bioluminescence in the ocean, perhaps it was "Light"?

13 In this case, silence is the universe enacting.

14 "Did Gertrude attempt communication with the Great Light?" "Did she feel her way through the dialectic of Light and Dark?" "Did she have her own felt structures the equivalent of the lantern fish and their silly bacterial communities longing to be free?" We footnoters concur that these were probably meant to be rhetorical questions.

15 For an individual construct to think of itself as an object independent of its surroundings à la Ayn Rand is about as intelligent as the bacteria bemoaning the stalking fish. It

cannot be a bacterial colony without its lantern. Without the fish the bacteria is like the heat produced by the toaster once the toaster is unplugged.

16 What this part of THE TEXT is really saying: relative silence can be found in the body because it is aLinguistic. This idea is the equivalent of the bacterial colony recognizing that it is an emergent phenomenon of the fish it has lately lambasted. There is a humility in that recognition that (with some effort) might lead to even greater social encephalization, or at least the footnoters assume this is the A-C's intent behind the passage.

17 If it weren't so cheeky we footnoters would proclaim (on behalf of the authorial construct) "Hypotheses non fingo!"

18 The eTEXT is primarily silent. Embedded and obligitory vocalizations are one exception.

19 Deep time as a term in this paragraph references: "A garden / of flight paths, verdant budding, and human napping, / the pattern cannot be picked apart; shadow / is still a compound verb, a progressive enactment / of light. This frail grey my fingers make, / this crow's wing, / that locust thorn and daisy / chain us all to slide tumbling into a green eternity.

20 The eTEXT engages in spatial and temporal displacement (aka movement) but always matches its sensed locus with the center of the universe. With the vast bulk of the eTEXT sensorium located in proximity to soma (in fact identical with soma), this seems largely unavoidable. It remains to be seen whether externally deposited conceptual frameworks (usually related to language or some other symbolic construct that can take material form, e.g. algorithms) can extend the reach of the primate sensorium and thus dislodge the currently bound relationship between "self" and somatic placement.

21 Simply put, soma moves through the world encoding. This is self-in-relation. This is also **thing**-in-relation. The reality simulator in the enclosed environment of the brain is limited by the material configuration of the various sense organs. It is that very configuration which makes the simulation effective as the organism moves through the world. The "limitations" are spatially, temporally and materially representative of the relationship between the organism's type, its environment, and its presence in deep time.

22 The total body of perceived "code" is vast even in the face of the seemingly infinite possibilities beyond soma's capabilities.

23 Foundationalism, as a philosophical position, (like the philosophical fundamentalism described in this section of THE TEXT) is an another attempt to make **thing**s stay still or to define **thing**-not-in-relation. We understand, but cannot muster much compassion.

24 A question that remains unanswered by the eTEXT – in the face of human reaction to whirling beauty, why aren't words enough to to create pockets of perceptual stillness?

25 A grandmother named Stanley. This footnoter admits to a mild snorting giggle.

26 Referenced here: "The hominid desire to befriend, or at least understand, the silence" (personal communication).

27 Full quote: "This is more than a metaphor; epileptic activity may in fact be among the most primitive of all functional states, given that it is so very similar across differeing species and different people. and independent of social and environmental factors. It is a bit like coughing or sneezing in this regard" (Llinás, p. 63).

[28] We concur. We do live and think without words. Of course there all those cognitively normal aLinguistic adults, who often for reasons of social isolation from signed languages combined with deafness from infancy, grow to a useful adulthood but without the particular conceptual frame which is language. In those of us who are linguistic, we have all those behavioural sets which do the majority of the thinking work for us as we move along. For those of us who have language it is just much harder to pay attention to them. That tin whistle we got as infants is LOUD.

[29] We admit the idea that visual art of the Lascaux kind suggests a shift from processual spatial reasoning (represented by the Willendorf figures) to a displaced-eye form of object-centred spatial reasoning (represented by the animal figures and hands painted on the walls of Dordogne caves. Our primate, it is suggested, has made the leap from continuous time/space that is inherent within communication to the notion of a discrete portions of time and space – a "here" and "there" conceptualization. They have achieved, mathematically speaking, a number line conception of reality. This ability to break down the world of self and nonself into bits does, in fact, seem to be the foundation of linguistic perception. In other words it is the creation of the bounded entity called a noun and the supression of the process called the field-of-**things**-in-relation.

[30] By this, the silence of **things** is spatially articulated in multiple geometries. It is clear that each constitutes an absoltue by contextual enactment.

[31] The yellow light of evening / it's like that ... / ... a fractured Tiffany lamp forever settling, / earth and her dragonflies / viridian moments pinned to silk gauze / these, interlaced by the distinctions—you & I— / and

this—under the evening's picture / all of us, pigment, mineral, aglimmer

gnOme is a secret press specializing in the publication of anonymous, pseudepigraphical, and apocryphal works from the past, present, and future.

"Listen to me, listen to the silence. What I say to you is never what I say to you but something else instead. It captures the thing that escapes me and yet I live from it and am above a shining darkness" (CL).

gnOme is acephalic. Book sales support the authors.

GNOMEBOOKS.WORDPRESS.COM

Other titles from gnOme

A & N • *Autophagiography*
Brian O'Blivion • *Blackest Ever Hole*
Eva Clanculator • *Atheologica Germanica*
M.O.N. • *ObliviOnanisM*
Pseudo-Leopardi • *Cantos for the Crestfallen*
Rasu-Yong Tugen, Baroness De Tristeombre • *Songs from the Black Moon*
Y.O.U. • *How to Stay in Hell*
M • *Un-Sight/ Un-Sound (delirium X.)*

HWORDE
Nab Saheb and Denys X. Arbaris • *Bergmetal: Oro-Emblems of the Musical Beyond*
Yuu Seki • *Serial Kitsch*
Doktor Faustroll • *An Ephemeral Exegesis on Crystalline Abrasions*

Made in the USA
Middletown, DE
01 February 2016